Once
I was
a little
boy.

Fredrick R. Abrams

Autobiography | Personal Memoirs

ISBN-10: 1977820298
ISBN-13: 978-1977820297

DEDICATION

My wife and constant partner and I have been together since 1947, then married in 1949. She never knew of the mischievous little boy of these true stories - until I wrote them. Despite Alice's discovery that I had burnt down my house when I was four, we are still together. Our sons, Reid, Glenn and Hal, have always been intrigued at our history so, of course, I dedicate this book to her and our three sons.

Once I Was a Little Boy

True Childhood Adventures

This is a series of stories about true adventures I had as a curious young boy, frequently exploring and experimenting in the world that surrounded me. I was born in 1928 so you must bear with me when I describe a much smaller world than the very wide one with which many readers today are familiar. The earliest experience I recall occurred when I was just between 4 and 5 years old. My two older brothers, Monny and Morty, were respectively 2 and 8 years older than me. Monny, being closer in age, was the more frequent co-conspirator in the several adventures I'm about to describe. Even though they occurred long before I was an adult, I must use my current vocabulary because these adventures are all retrospective escapades and my memory can no longer be that only of a child between 4 and 14.

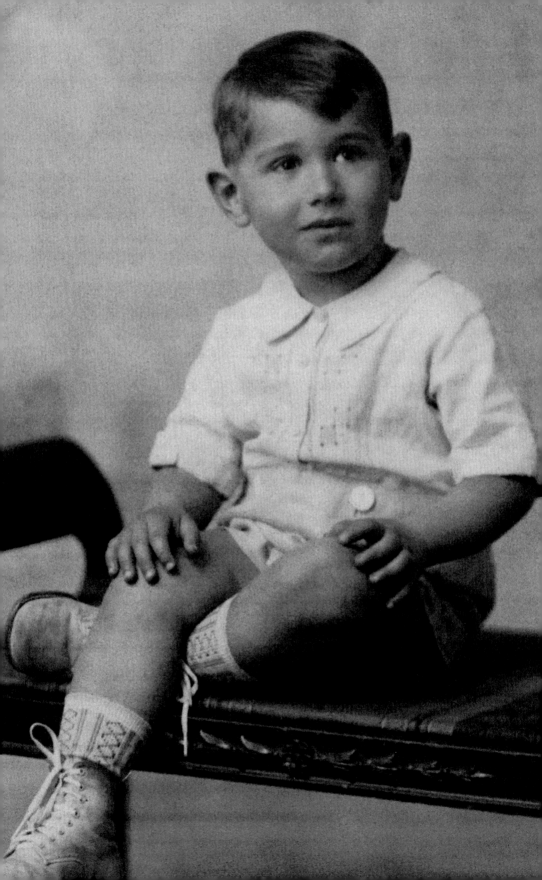

TABLE OF CONTENTS

Now the true tale of that snowy winter afternoon can be told, when I was four and Monny was six. It was then that we two had called upon the four ancient elements - air, earth (snow-covered), water and (house-consuming) fire, but the newspaper and fire department substituted instead "faulty chimney wires."

Yes, there were two pups in our true memory. Only my brother survived the fractures when he and doggy-one fell from our porch together. Our next pal, Pal, lived with us for decades, playing football, baseball, wrestling, running - everything, until one sad day.

My mother tolerated but did not appreciate my collection of insects and small animals - especially the thousands of spiders that once found their way to the kitchen. But it was my big BIG brother that truly appreciated my small painted friend that won him a prize.

Although hot dogs and French fries always came first, two unfortunate events followed at Atlantic Beach. At age four, there was a barber with no talent and dull scissors. A few years later, I shouted twice (in eight-year old language) "Get me off of this dumb horse!"

Especially before antibiotics, the family doctor would visit because pneumonia was serious business. I survived but it was not only because of chicken soup. It was one of very few illnesses that could keep me from Saturday afternoon movies where the Weekly Newsreel, the "Chapters" with prizes for winners, the cartoons and finally the double feature climaxed the day (plus Jujubes, Black Crows, Peanut Brittle or Mr. Goodbar).

Monny and I felt abandoned for the Thanksgiving feast when we were separated far from the adult dining room table. Turkey-napping was the alternative.

A Good Humor man drove into our garage and joined my big Big brother, Morty, in a poker game. Upstairs, middle brother Monny, was in bed suffering from poison oak and smeared with pink calamine lotion. Could I snag (just for the two of us) multiple boxes of butterscotch-coffee ice cream from a locked truck?

Mr. Guttmann and his wife owned a candy store that my friends and I visited almost daily after school. Much to our surprise there were two police cars at the curb and the sign inside the door said "CLOSED."

When I came home from school and my usual cookies and milk were not on the kitchen table I called out, "Mom!" Hearing no reply I hastened to the front of the house where I found mom lying on the couch. She appeared to be sleeping.

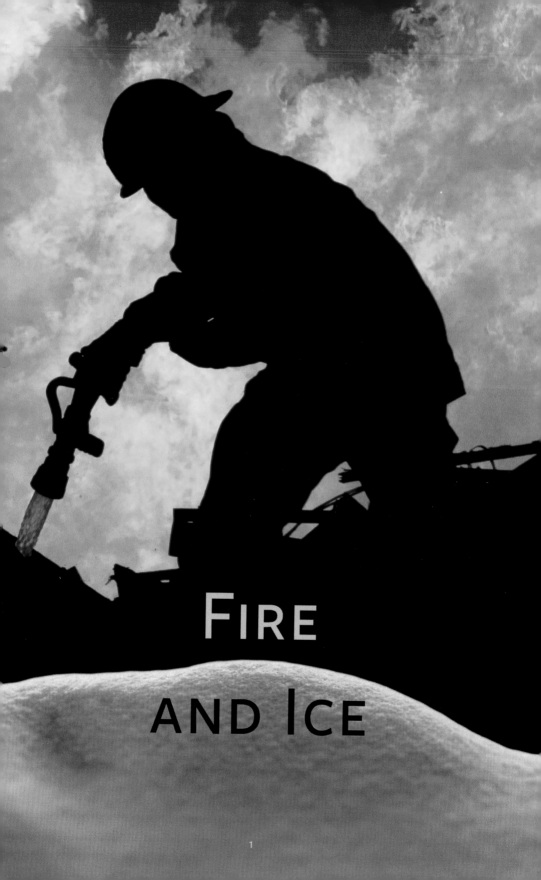

FIRE

AND ICE

FIRE AND ICE

After the misadventure had happened I was a few years older and able to read much better. It was then that I came upon the headline and the news story that dad had clipped from the local newspaper and kept in his desk. I read the first page where the headlines screamed:

3 FOOT SNOW BARS FIRETRUCKS
3-STORY HOME TOTAL LOSS

Faulty chimney wires started a blaze in the snowbound house at 343 Summit Avenue yesterday afternoon. Fire trucks, delayed by the deep snow, found the hydrant frozen when they finally arrived just in time to watch the house burn to a total loss.

Oh, had they only known!

Now, close to 84 years later, I can recall and relate the story without risk of a spanking. Then I was four and a half years old and my big brother was a full six and a half. That wintry day the snow was so deep that school was closed for him. I had not yet matriculated to kindergarten.

Kitchen, parlor, dining and living rooms were ensconced on the first floor of our three-story house along with the live-in maid's room. In the early 1930s a maid was not an unusual member of many middle class households. Our second floor held three bedrooms and two whole baths! But the third floor was the magic floor for my brother and me. It was virtually empty and therefore a wide-open playroom with dormer windows from which we could spy upon whatever action was passing in the

3

street. True, it had a slanted ceiling but this was disregarded because neither of us had stature sufficient to offer a challenge, even to the lowest corners.

What space we did not occupy with sundry toys became storage for various household goods. In the 1930s, seasonal weather variations were acknowledged by changes in furnishings. The hardwood floors of the rooms in winter were covered with large rugs – no wall-to-wall carpet in those days. Rather a single large fringed rug of oriental design in the living room supplied many ornate twisted roadways along which I could drive my toy mini-cars. Periodic floral designs served us there as gas stations or restaurants, where I stopped for imaginary refreshments when my arms grew tired of pushing the toys along the convoluted highway.

Much like our clothing, for which there were winter and summer outfits, so too in the summer, straw rugs replaced these heavy woolen carpets. They lightened the atmosphere and seemed to make the humid summer air less oppressive. Air conditioners in homes were just beginning and certainly a rarity of that era. Preparations were made as winter approached by adding storm windows over the single panes of glass of which windows were constructed at that time. The sequential changing of the carpets followed as the next sign that ushered in the cold weather. The winter carpets were brought down from the third floor, where they had reposed adjacent to our toys, and the straw rugs took back their rightful place, once more to rest until spring welcomed them back into the living areas downstairs.

Thus conspired the fates for the conflagration immortalized in the headlines.

On any ordinary snowy day, we might have found ourselves in snowsuits a few blocks from home on Leroy Avenue. There several friends had the good fortune of residing on a street with a long gentle downhill slope. With our Flexible Flyer sleds, we spent many hours sliding down and then trekking back up the hill until setting sun called us home. In that era it was perfectly safe for kids to wander a few blocks from home because adults kept an eye out for all the children, even offering a thermos with hot cocoa poured into paper cups to neighborhood kids. But on this day, the snow was still falling and much too deep to allow such ventures. Brother and I repaired to the third floor playroom.

No doubt about it, I was precocious! But not quite enough – and that's what got us into trouble. That afternoon my brother and I took out our little metal toy cars and raced them. No motors of any kind existed in such toys as today's advanced technology might provide. Ours didn't even have wind-up springs. We raced using only small boy push power as we verbalized our roaring motors RRRRRRrrrrrrrRRRRRR-RRRR. Soon, racing across an open hard wood floor became boring and our eyes fell upon the rolled up straw carpets. They were perfect tunnels. Side by side they reposed and now a vigorous push sped the cars through. Only at the last moment as they emerged would we know who won. Alas! The muscle power of my brother's two-year growth advantage made him the consistent winner. It was then I pondered upon what had made my father's car operate – oil! Could I employ this fuel to accelerate my vehicle so it would out-speed my big brother's? I recalled there were several oilcans on a shelf in the garage, but it was a building separate from the house, and to my chagrin, inaccessible through the deep snow.

Recalling that dad had fixed the squeaky hinge on the kitchen door with a can of 3-in-one oil and had left it conveniently under the sink, we agreed that fuel could be the answer to my prayers. We raced to the kitchen, passing the maid who was preparing milk and cookies for our usual 3:00 O'clock snack. Grasping the oilcan we sped back to the third floor. Soon we learned that squirting oil under the toy car's hood merely poured it through the vehicle's empty bottom (and inadvertently onto the straw rug). What could keep it in the engine compartment? With some difficulty and the use of little boy's teeth, we tore off a corner from my handkerchief and saturated it well with viscous oil. Now we must remind you of what had been (beside the hand crank) an essential part of starting the early motorcars that my father drove – it was the spark!

On rare occasions I had been privileged to sit on dad's lap, pretending to drive, while vainly struggling with the steering wheel that I could barely move in the immobile vehicle. With the key turned off, he had allowed me to pull the handles and twist the dials that in early autos were placed in the center of the steering wheel. One, he told me, was called the choke and the other was the spark. They both sounded funny to me. Who would be choked or why could only be speculated upon – but it was the spark that captured my imagination!

On July 4th each year we saw fireworks, including some that exploded spectacularly. But we were not allowed these loud and somewhat dangerous noisemakers. Instead we had to be contented with SPARKlers. These were wires coated with material that, once ignited, burned brightly as we waved them in the air, but they did not explode. I made the tenuous connection with sparklers to my nascent automotive project. The spark lever on the steering wheel, I thought, had something to do with igniting the fuel that propelled the car. I knew that if my car was to move through the carpet tunnel, it needed a spark.

By now my brother had been enthusiastically drawn into this experiment and was eager to supply the missing ingredient – matches! He knew where dad kept them, on his desk next to his cigars. This was to be a venture into a truly forbidden zone but nothing could stop two budding engineers from what appeared to be an achievable solution to the challenging problem of self-propulsion – an auto-mobile!

We craftily crept to the forbidden cigar and match site, secured the contraband and dashed back to the racetrack where we had lined up two oil and handkerchief laden vehicles, placed half inside the straw rug tunnels. To be certain of fairness and an even start to the race, we ignited the torn cloths simultaneously and gave each a gentle push further into the tunnels. At precisely that moment we heard the irresistible summons from the kitchen, "cookies and milk." Unable to ignore that temptation, we scurried downstairs thinking how magic it would be to find our vehicles at the far end of the rug tunnels when we returned.

After the hastily consumed treats, we went to the bottom of the staircase, ready to ascend and see if our plans for vehicular mobility had materialized. Rapidly it became apparent that something had gone wrong. We were met by a strong smoky odor. We recalled that it resembled the smoke from the burning piles of leaves we had raked each autumn within which we roasted potatoes snatched from the kitchen. Aware that all was not well because no potatoes had been available, we climbed a few steps from the bottom landing to where we could see further up the inclined stairway. There we saw thick black smoke pouring down the staircase.

Dashing back to the kitchen again, we found the wash bucket under the sink. Bucket filling appeared to be a novel bit of mischief by the children that the maid had not previously observed. All too often she had seen us inventing varieties of activities, often with undesirable consequences, so she inquired about our plans. Scarcely pausing to inform the maid that there appeared to be some source of smoke from upstairs, the two of us together barely succeeded to lift the heavy half-full bucket of water. We managed to spill most of it en route to the staircase. With great teamwork and significant giggling we heaved the contents straight up the stairway but the remainder of the liquid obeyed the law of gravity, and descending downward, thoroughly saturated the two of us.

The maid, who had followed us, quickly discerned that something dangerous was afoot. Wasting not a moment on trivialities, nor to be mistaken in priority, she swiftly ran to the birdcage where our treasured canary appeared to have succumbed, much as in the toxic fabled coal mines. Unhooking the cage from its stand, she rescued the moribund bird by dashing out the door through the snow-filled yard to the neighbor's house, and there raised the alarm.

Brother and I managed another half-bucketful; again with a sodden failure to defy gravity before the neighbor lady next door arrived. We relinquished the bucket regretfully as she pulled us from the smoke filled environment. She did not appear to appreciate whatever it was that precipitated the uncontrollable giggling from the two of us as we struggled through several feet of snow to her house.

There, we were vigorously buffed and swathed in large bath towels, not unlike the ancient Roman togas. Peering through the frosted window, we witnessed the belated arrival of the firemen, their search and ultimate uncovering of the buried hydrant, followed by the failure of the unreeled frozen hose to fill, as we watched our house sprout flames. Our home and all we possessed was doomed, with the exception of the resuscitated canary, which apparently had waxed temperamental and not surprisingly, refused to cheer us with song. At that time, I regretted most the loss of my Tom Mix cowboy suit complete with chaps, ten-gallon hat and six-shooter cap pistol that were in the cupboard on the second floor. Only in retrospect, a sad truth revealed itself to me – it would have been better had I stayed with the cowboy persona and the horse itself, the historical conveyance of that era, rather than the horseless carriage we had attempted to motorize.

Did we ever relate to anyone our fateful encounter with the combustible character of the internal combustion engine? No – indeed not. No one ever inquired about our activities prior to the fire so we never had to fabricate. In fact, we received much sympathy and affection, having escaped the twin threat of fire and ice. We knew, even in those tender years, never to volunteer incriminating activities. Many subsequent escapades, the remainder of which I can honestly characterize only as annoying but actually harmless mischief, never approached the gravity of this inadvertent destruction. Now the true tale of that cold winter afternoon can be told, when we called upon three of the four ancient elements – air, fire and water – lacking only snow-covered earth, because the newspaper and fire department substituted instead "faulty chimney wires."

A TALE OF TWO
PUPPIES

A TALE OF TWO PUPPIES

To describe the French revolution, the oft-quoted scene composed by Charles Dickens started with, "It was the best of times." Our tale of two puppies began that way but followed all too soon with the rest of his quotation, "It was the "worst of times." This is a facsimile of two such sequential events although they occurred hundreds of years later with canines.

When my brother Monny and I (he being the elder) were 10 and 12 years of age we began our petition because we absolutely needed a dog. We gave our most solemn pledge (offered with left hand over heart and right raised palm forward) offering our "word of honor" that we would feed him, water him, walk him, toilet train him – everything that might persuade parents that every family with small boys needed a dog. We maintained it would be good for everyone and then, as trumps, we played the "responsibility" card. Wouldn't it teach us responsibility and dissuade us from mischief, deeds that had never been done with evil intent but simply out of sheer boredom?

Truly, we didn't know what turned the tide, but persistent begging suddenly returned results! Perhaps we had been unusually well behaved – or possibly so mischievous that mother felt we needed distraction, but one Sunday dad told us to jump into the car. We were going to the "Bide a Wee Home" that served as the orphanage for dogs and cats abandoned on Long Island.

Once there we perused the large spaces surrounded with high wire fences that enclosed the huddled masses yearning to be free. Just as we Americans have more recently been classified as mongrels, there were dogs that were the very essence of miscegenation with their wide varieties of virtually unlimited size, color, shape and temperament. Our family held no prejudice regarding origins. We could trace our own forebears only three generations. Soon we claimed a small pup with wooly fur and wistful eye that scampered into our arms and appeared very happy to escape the motley pack of canines with whom he shared living quarters. The breed was up for grabs, said the attendant, speculating this might be the consequence of a female Pomeranian that was ravaged by a toy poodle during a night on the town.

Mom and dad, who initially had appeared so open hearted, cruelly refused to let the puppy sleep with us that night. Vainly, we pointed out that there was ample room in either of our twin beds. They explained that first and foremost a defleaing trip to the vet was essential. The poor pup, deposited on a blanket in a basket on the basement landing, serenaded us all night with a mournful doggy dirge. I'm sure that led our parents to regret the canine acquisition in its entirety. When brother and I went downstairs at the very first crack of dawn, so happy was he to see us on that bright summer morning that he leapt up as high as his short legs could carry him, licking all and any hands, feet and faces that he could access.

We had a brick house with a driveway that ran alongside the porch. The wide front porch sported cushioned Adirondack chairs suitable for lounging on summer evenings to watch traffic or passersby on the street. Around the porch periphery there was a narrow brick wall, perhaps three feet high, with spaces placed symmetrically such that small boys squatting could peer through. The three-foot porch wall was necessary to protect people from falling the ten feet from the porch to the adjacent concrete driveway alongside and below.

To the front porch we went, brother, puppy and I, very early on that warm summer morning. I don't know what possessed my brother but he seized the as yet unnamed pup, and using the spaces in the brick wall as a ladder, stepped onto the top and began the tightrope traverse to the stairway at the end. I shouted at him to come back down onto the porch – fearful that he might drop the dog, but he scornfully continued his daredevil performance. The puppy, of the same mind as I, began to squirm frantically. Trying to retain his balance as well as holding the wriggling and panicky pup was too much for Monny and over the wall they went together to the concrete driveway over ten feet below.

Running down the steps to find both of them crying painfully, I only had eyes for the poor victim with the broken leg – the dog of course. Paired fractures were the ultimate diagnoses but at that time I had no sympathy for the bearer of the broken arm, my brother. Dad, just getting ready to go to work and drawn by the cries of distress, appeared. Quickly, he assessed the situation, and noting the impossible angle of my brother's arm, shouted a few words to my mother and took Monny in the car to St. Joseph's Hospital. Mom called upon our neighbor, also readying for work, to drive my 18-year- old big BIG brother with the dog to the vet, a trip that did not include me.

Reconstructing the situation now, big BIG brother had left with clandestine instructions for the veterinarian. Spending money on a mutt (not an appellation of my appreciation) was beyond the pale. Mercy killing was the common solution. Learning that "the dog had died," was certainly true, but without the dastardly details. Knowing where the responsibility lay for the dual catastrophe, my ten year-old sense of justice might have had a difficult time deciding which patient should have had the bone set. Luckily, in the heat of the moment the decision had not been left to me. But a few days later, when Monny was struggling with the cast of heavy plaster (the only type of material that was available in that era) and knowing his activity was to be limited for weeks, plus the grimace from his obvious discomfort, appeared to be punishment enough. Regretting my evil thoughts, especially in light of all we already had survived together, it was only a foreshadowing of the adventures to come.

Learning soon how quickly we forget, along came Pal. It was almost a year later that our fickle hearts admitted there was room for another comrade of the canine persuasion. Pal was a more mature four-legged friend who was passed on to us by a nearby family that was moving from our town. They regretted that they couldn't include their pet in the complicated journey involved in their transition. He was an affable pet, mostly sheepdog, and coming from a family with several small children, seemed to enjoy the roughhousing play to which he was subjected by us. But for our parents, the clincher was that he was already toilet trained.

Initially, mom disapproved of her sons sharing beds with a dog. We assumed it was doubtlessly some inherent fastidiousness that was gender-specific. To encourage nocturnal separation and thinking she had a better chance of convincing Pal than us of her position, she had provided him with a nest of an old soft flannel blanket in a snug box just inside the back door of the house. But an even warmer facility, preferred by dogs and children alike, were our beds. There was, however, an obstacle to overcome – our bedroom door. Mom insisted we close it – usually reluctantly – when we retired to our bedroom for the night with the intention of excluding four-footed visitors. Somehow our bedroom door never latched securely. Ultimately mom abandoned her insistence on separate sleeping quarters as a hopeless task. Pal seemed happy in whoever's bed he was sharing that particular night.

Pal enjoyed reading. Well, not exactly. He enjoyed it when we were reading on the couch. Mom had adjudged the couch forbidden territory for Pal, were he to venture on it unescorted. But, if one of us were reading quietly there, he would climb up and put his head in our lap and rest. This frequent violation was overlooked because mom didn't want to risk the few quiet moments in her life when boys and dog were not involved in any visible mischief. There was one other thing that was sure to disturb the peaceable kingdom. Should someone approach the front door anytime of day or night and have the temerity to ring the bell, a large ball of fur that surrounded a flurry of furious barking would hurtle toward the door. Certainly that discouraged many door-to-door salesmen from putting a foot in the door.

All three brothers continued the tradition of interspecies wrestling matches, often a melee of four souls unable ever to pin the furriest of us down. He could squirm away from any hold we tried, never once growling or baring his teeth. But the most formal athletic endeavor in which he participated was football practice for our seven-gladiator team, "The Freckled Goldfish." When we needed practice in running and tackling, we assembled in the vacant lot across the street with a rag doll we had acquired.

After lining up in full football regalia, consisting of hi-topped canvas sneakers, miscellaneous sweatshirts, old knickers or blue jeans and the only element of a football uniform we all owned – helmets, we would give the doll to Pal who faced the team. Holding it in his mouth, he would pin it to the ground between his extended forelegs and gaze up to see who would be first to make a grab for it. He could not be bluffed by sudden false starts, but when someone crossed the line – a line apparent only to Pal – he would snatch it up and dodge to any of the four points of the compass. No one could touch him, let alone capture the stand-in football – the rag doll.

He had another trait that was in all likelihood an atavistic remnant of his sheepdog forebears. If the members of our team scattered too widely across the vacant lot, he would circle the outliers, yapping with determination while nudging them together until we were once again bunched together in a lineup proper for football – or shearing – whichever activity Pal considered was to be next on the schedule.

Pal became something of a problem in baseball season. Generally, we played a variant called stickball. The equipment was comprised of a sawed off broomstick and a few tennis balls, generally called "spaldeens." Later I realized this was an eastern linguistic corruption of the "Spalding" trademark. Here Pal had an intellectual failing. He was unable to identify and distinguish the appropriate games for the various seasons. He considered the "spaldeen" baseball challenge identical with the catch-me-if-you-can football practice. Any free ball hit to the infield or outfield was up for grabs – and he was the most talented grabber. Many a game was called – or at least temporarily delayed – because of a captured ball. That was why we resorted to keeping several on hand. Any Pal-captured ball was an automatic double by local ground rules. We knew it was fruitless to try to retrieve it from a dog with a find-ers-keepers attitude.

Several happy years of canine companionship continued as we all grew up together. We spent time playing baseball and football, crab hunting in the nearby inlets and lowlands bordering the Atlantic Ocean, chasing seagulls and never catching them and salvaging golf balls for resale from the wade-able waterholes in local golf cours-es. Often Pal explored widely and independently during the day while we were at school. There were no leash laws then, and anyway, Pal was everyone's pal. Also, he had a good sense of timing because he would usually show up at home shortly after we returned from school, knowing there were cookies and milk that we surrepti-tiously shared.

One sunny morning, just as summer vacation began, Pal left early for his customary survey and territorial claim of hydrants and telephone poles. We didn't think much about it when his absence became extended. Perhaps, we speculated, he thinks we're still away at school most of the day. Monny and I became occupied with other things. Morty, my big BIG brother had long since followed other pursuits more suit-able for his advanced age – after all, he was eight years older than me. But when six o'clock came and Pal had not visited his two water bowls, inside or outside, we be-came concerned and decided to scout the neighborhood.

Where our home street, Maple Avenue, crossed the towns main street, Central Av-enue, the Rensey drugstore stood at the corner intersection. We were frequent customers (invariably accompanied by Pal) because the proprietor, Mr. Yesner (NB: Rensey spelled backward) also had an ice cream soda fountain. We poked our heads in the door and asked Mr. Yesner if Pal had come his way. Most of the time he would chat with us about what we were learning at school or about his son, away at col-lege. This time he appeared unusually hesitant to talk with us. He was fussing with a prescription, so we just stood there, waiting for an answer. Then he said something like, "Well, there was an accident earlier this afternoon – I'm pretty sure."

"Sure of what, Mr. Yesner," I asked.

"Well a dog was hit by a car and was hurt badly, and," he paused.

"And what," I asked, beginning to panic.

"The dog was hurt so badly that the cop shot him – it was the right thing to do."

"Was it Pal?"

Then Mr. Yesner said, "I'm sorry," and that answered the question.

Hurrying to the nearby police station, the two of us were woefully hoping there was a mistake. We asked the policeman at the desk if he knew anything about a dog being shot. Asking us to wait a minute he stepped into the back room. Then he came out bringing Pal's collar. We never learned of his disposition. Someone once said, "Big boys don't cry," but we weren't so big, after all.

That evening in my basement workshop, I tacked to the wall a photo we had made of Pal, scrunched down over the rag doll in the lot across the street, ready to scrimmage. Then, with a wood-burning pen that we used to outline pictures on small scraps of plywood we printed:

The Pal
Memorial

In memory
of a best friend.

Under that we angle-ironed a small shelf. My plan was to have an eternal light candle burning on the shelf but Monny reminded me of the catastrophic consequences the last time we had left an untended flame burning and we prudently substituted a flashlight. The PAL MEMORIAL remained there until we moved four years later.

BIG BROTHER

AND MY CREATURE COLLECTION

BIG BROTHER
AND MY
CREATURE COLLECTION

As the youngest of three sons, my two big brothers were alternately a burden and a blessing. It was years later that I appreciated how they truly were a blessing, but not in my early immature years as the youngest and smallest of the boys. My most frequent burden occurred at dinner when the main course was served from a large platter in mid-table. Longer arms were a distinct advantage for the larger carnivores. My middle brother was two years older, close enough in age to be competitive. But the big BIG brother's birthdate preceded mine by eight years. Unlike big brother, my big BIG brother barely noticed me, tolerating me merely as a petty annoyance, until the memorable day I won an esteemed place in his field of honor. This was no small thing for I was but a lowly fourth grader while he was a glorious high school senior.

A little background is necessary. Whenever anything with four to six legs chanced my way, collecting insects and small fauna made me something of an early naturalist. There was a celebrity of the 1930s calling himself "Frank Buck" who provided zoos and circuses with many different animals. He promoted his menagerie with the motto, *Bring 'em Back Alive*. Having neither the skill nor means to mimic that great outdoorsman, my success was on a much smaller scale, having brought back alive (to my basement) a motley collection of frogs, salamanders and a turtle. I was a little disappointed that they did not socialize well with my insects because they preferred to dine upon the six-legged species rather than establishing friendships.

My laboratory cum workshop was a room in the basement adjoining the former coal bin that had recently been rendered obsolete. No longer did a huge truck back into our driveway and groaningly tilt its coal-laden bed, allowing the fuel to slide down a narrow window chute into the cellar while clouds of coal dust besmirched the atmosphere inside and outside the house.

No longer hypnotized by the glowing fire pit, as my dad or BIG brother formerly shoveled chunks of coal through the furnace door to heat the house in the cold months. We had modernized by converting the furnace to an oil burner. Feeling the loss immediately, no longer able to display my latent artistic ability as a founding member of a burgeoning, if little known school of art, substituting anthracite for palette knife or brush, and therewith scraping black graffiti on the sidewalk or neighboring brick walls.

The basement was also a source of many specimens for research. Few members of my household were as enthusiastic about these endeavors. Mom tolerated but did not appreciate my insect and animal collection. Particularly admiring crickets but unable ever to encourage them to chirp once captured, I simply sat noiselessly admiring their talent. Soon I learned that they were not vocalizing but rather rubbing their legs together rhythmically. Again this was a disappointment to me. Not that I disapproved, but primarily because rubbing my stocking covered shins together as hard as I might, I failed to duplicate anything that could imitate the chirps.

One of my happiest discoveries was the innumerable little brown sacs suspended in countless spider webs in basement corners. I immediately suspected they were spider eggs – not precisely true but close enough to take me to the next level of creativity. I collected them in a glass jelly jar, amassing scores of them over several days and set them on my worktable of wooden slatted orange crates salvaged from the grocery store. On one triumphant day when I returned from school at three-thirty to view my collection, I was rewarded by a half pint jar swarming with thousands of pinhead-sized infant spiders that had emerged from the round and flexible varied size sacs!

Absolutely thrilled by my successful venture into the reproductive arts, and snatching the jar teeming with wonderful mini-arthropods, I flew up the stairs to the kitchen, shouting "Mom, mom, look what I have." Now mother knew I had various collections in my basement laboratory but had shielded herself from details that she felt were in all likelihood harmless but not exactly her cup of tea. She was busily occupied near the kitchen sink preparing food for dinner, so to get her attention and approval too, I held the jar up to her face as she indulgently deigned to look at whatever I was proudly offering.

Only a short time later thinking back on this occasion, my conclusion was that she was indeed impressed, because as the jar approached her visual field she emitted a sudden shriek unlike anything I had ever heard from my mother before – or since. In turn this was quite alarming to me. My firm grip on the spider receptacle created a startle-reflex, snapping open my hand and thus releasing the former jelly container to the unyielding linoleum floor. If a container of entrapped spiders elicited such a reaction from mother, I leave it to your imagination what the consequence was of shattered glass and thousands of freedom-loving spiders scattering in all directions.

Fortunately there was a chair nearby and mom, no longer so close to syncope, took sanctuary there with her legs raised to the supportive rungs. Heartbroken because my collection would have been unrivaled by any one at P.S.#3, my coup at "show and tell" was thwarted. Pointing to the broom and dustpan before retiring to the parlor for the necessary recuperation, mom assigned the task to me to sweep away all of the shards and fleeing spiders. Reassembling the cache was hopeless because of the spider's admirable mobility added to their minute size, as well as the absence of additional empty jelly jars. Mother showed no remorse for destroying my entomological feat and thwarting my potential moment of classroom triumph.

Now you shall see how these apparent digressions truly relate to my moment of fraternal jubilation. One of my most recent acquisitions was a house mouse that had been seduced by an odorous portion of moldy cheese that had baited a basement trap. The trap was one among many set in the cellar. Cautionary action had been precipitated by a frightening episode reported by my mother. She had encountered this very mouse (or a member of his family) while conveying clothes to be laundered in the basement tubs. Washboards of corrugated metal and wood were immersed in warm soapy water over which dirty clothes were rubbed in dual sinks, one for washing, one to rinse. This technique preceded the labor saving devices later known as washing machines.

Having barely recovered from the spider episode, mom left the disposition of the deceased rodent to me. Briefly considering there might be a mouse heaven because Mickey and Minnie, who had many humanoid features, had entranced my entire generation - nevertheless collecting the mouse and resetting the trap seemed proper. Of course, I pondered the best future for this mouse that had spiritually gone to its eternal reward, and kept it in my workshop with ice cubes temporarily until I could determine, within reasonable time limits, whether it could have earthly value, or would need proper burial.

The weekend was upon us. To me that had the meaning only of respite from school. To my big BIG brother however, it was party time. In those days there was a festivity that now I hear little of in contemporary teen activities. It was a scavenger hunt! A group of partygoers would be divided into teams. Each team would be given the same list of somewhat exotic items to acquire in a limited time. The team that gathered the most would receive the prize. Today, many teens might not be willing to arise and scavenge for less than a Mac computer for each, but then free tickets to the Movies at 25 cents each sufficed. The list of items to be acquired might include an Indian head penny, a Japanese fan, a tuxedo jacket, an autographed baseball, red pajamas, a Glenn Miller record, a Mickey Mouse watch, last Sunday's comic strip- you get the idea.

Curled up in my favorite chair and reading a Big Little Book, suddenly my big BIG brother and a cortege of friends dashed through the door. Apparently he had not been totally unaware of my esoteric talents. Breathlessly he told me that his team had acquired everything on a scavenger hunt list except – a white mouse! That, once acquired, would make him a sure winner. Of course, that would also make a hero of me and in all his friends' eyes, of him – especially because he had assured them that if anyone could produce a white mouse it would be his little brother.

Announcing that such an item could be provided but with one small problem, the cadaver in my possession was a dull gray. That would not stop a necromancer from fulfilling a request from so august a solicitor as his big BIG brother. Demonstrating the furry corpse and bidding the anxious partygoers to wait a few moments, then rushing to the upstairs bathroom, I uncovered from the cabinet under the sink a precious bottle. The substance therein was the secret to scavenging success – white liquid shoe polish!

Dunking the specimen into the liquid took only a moment as it dried in a washcloth. (The next day, questioned by mother, I feigned ignorance of the pallid cloth). Approaching the scavengers, reassured that mobility was not essential for the mouse they sought, all doubts were set aside. Revealing my prize to shouts of approval, the assemblage hastily departed. The next morning, my BIG brother thanked me profusely for his triumphant sortie of the previous evening and, mirabile dictu, wonders will never cease! My big BIG brother volunteered to take me to next Saturday's afternoon movie!

EIGHT POEMS

National Geographic
An Intrigin' Magazine

National Geographic – an intrigin' magazine
has fascinatin' stories
about places you ain't been

Showin' people from all over in different kinda clothes
also people shown all over
where their clothes are goodness knows!

Saw an interestin' story 'bout a wealthy English lord
huntin' lions in old India
(English colony abroad)

There were thirty native porters also servants and a cook
And they all lined up behind the lord
to have their pichers took

Out in front of them a lion stretched, appearin' bored
but the bullet holes and blood, they showed
he had gone to his reward

And the lord, he stood asmilin' for the home folks so they'd see
from the picher that he'd made there
he'd go down in history

Time has passed since that old photo, maybe sixty years or more
and it took that long before the lion
had to even up the score

That lion he must now be stuffed and hangin' on a wall
In the study that the English lord
Had called his trophy hall

Yes the lion has an honored place where all posterity
Can admire his toothy visage
In its ageless constancy

But the lord is buried somewhere,
formless features naught but dust
And the lion's in his study
If he knew that wouldn't he bust!!

Yes the lion's in his study and the lord is in the ground
Chances are no one can tell us where his coffin may be found
There's a lesson lurkin' somewhere if we studied it enough
But I'll turn the page on over and I'll look at other stuff

Wow! Here's some better pichers of some natives in the buff!

ALLITERATION GAME

Vigorously the busy bug vaulted over the verge
Of my footprint
In the simmering sand

To me each glittering grain seemed the same
At the side
Of the sighing sea

But the bug searchingly swept his sensitive
Feelers over each
Formidable facet

For each glassy mass was unlike
Any other world

And his progress pended perfect palpation of the particle

Are pits and pinnacles only distorting the surface
Of a constant core of truth?

Or, if truth is tenderly searched on all its sides
And surfaces
Do we find it is indeed inconstant?

When the sea scrubbed the sand
Serenely smooth again
Where did my footprint go?

THE PRAGMATIST AND IDEALIST OUT FOR A STROLL

Our crosswalk light was clearly seen

For us it was distinctly green

The truck bore down

I swallowed pride

And cravenly I jumped aside

In staunch defense of principle

He thought himself invincible

The final words I heard him say

"Fear not! We have the right of way."

THE UNIVERSE

On a galaxy that's whirling
On its swift and endless run
There's a planet spinning madly
'Round its slowly dying sun

On the planet there are oceans
And some land that's poking through
On the land there is a river
Flowing downward, as they do

Near the river there's a farmyard
With an irrigation ditch
And a puddle drying slowly
Since the farmer pulled the switch

On the edges of the puddle
There's a fringe of greenish slime
And some bugs were gathered 'round it
At this point in boundless time

They had gathered in the puddle
When they tired of buggy play
Since their lives were spent entirely
In this quickly passing day

There was vigorous debating
With much ranting, raving strife
For they all had raised the question
Of the meaning of their life

And one simple bug had shouted
"I can see no mystery
We're so smart to have created
Something wonderful as we"

"For aren't we the highest
And most complex form of thing
Our puddle is the universe
Come let our praises ring"

As they bent their heads together
In a smugly prideful bow
Their universe with all of them
Was stepped on by a cow

FREDRICK R. ABRAMS

FOUNDATIONS

Can anything grow without branches or roots

What nourishment comes from wax painted fruits

Can minds be protected from constant confusion

If the thinkers conceive all conception illusion

When a structure is formed from the fabric of dreams

One must build it on frameworks of mind-fancied beams

IDEAS

The earth convulsed and up thrust stone

Which stood for eons all alone

Ice capped it with a crystal crown

'Til wind and weather wore it down

Then slowly as it changed its shape

Trees covered it with verdant cape

And water carved across its face

Age lines of silver liquid lace

The mountain bathed in lunar light

Stands sentinel and guards the night

As timeless as it seems to be

It wears away so gradually

Someday no trace will yet remain

Where once was mountain will be plain

Those things you touch must cease to be

But ideas last eternally

VERSE FOR A MAN WITHOUT A SPACE BETWEEN HIS INCISORS

My shoes athwart the sidewalk slid

My eyes ideas questing

My mind reminding ruefully

My body bade me resting

PAUSE

Now is the time I've abandoned the strivings

Past are the days when I hastened tomorrow

Here in the sun of a golden December

I am content just to wonder and linger

Would I could halt the inexorable turning

Yet I must join the whole world in its journey

I've breathed the warm air of the slumbering summer

And chilled with the snow of the crisp and clear winter

I would not start over yet wish I could hover

From knowledge I've fled and I'm nearly at wisdom

I'm blessed with a life that's been filled with good fortune

Now I would
Look
Taste
Smell
Touch and
Listen

MISFORTUNES OF
OF
BOARDWALK
AND BEACH

MISFORTUNES OF BOARDWALK AND BEACH

On many summer Sundays, dad, mom, my two older brothers and I would jump into the Chevy and drive from our home that was close to the south shore of Long Island, alternating to different beaches on the sandy edges of the Atlantic Ocean. I was five, Monny was seven and Morty was thirteen.

Our adventures depended on the season, the weather and sometimes the presence of a boardwalk. At that time such walks had been built on only a few public beaches. On sunny, warm days we would sprawl on large beach towels between trips to the edges of the incoming foamy ocean. We splashed as the shallow waves came in and carefully dodged the intermittent high breakers. Only real swimmers went beyond the waves, providing it was a day calm enough to swim out on the often-placid ocean. We dug for clams, then threw them back and tried to catch other firm-shelled multi-legged creatures without much success as they dug rapidly down into the soft moist sand.

It was decades later as their years multiplied, that more pale white citizens realized the danger that the bright hot sun imposed on Caucasian skin. Only a few wise young ladies and even fewer men wore broad rimmed beach hats and stayed mostly under beach umbrellas. So-called suntan lotion was of varied protection until several years later when they added substances that progressively increased the protection from the sun's rays.

If it were a season too cool for the beach and ocean itself, dad would invest in a boardwalk ride in bi-wheeled vehicles actually pushed from behind by young men. A few years later, bicycles attached in front of such carriages became the more common mode of transport. Most of our family expeditions were pleasant sojourns but there were two undesirable experiences for the five, and then eight year-old me on the boardwalk and beach. Mom decided that Monny and I both needed haircuts and the adjacent barbershop alongside the boardwalk had a large sign announcing that children's haircuts were a special on Sunday. So, simultaneously we both climbed up onto the rotating and tilting leather-lined chairs. Our Italian barbers exchanged words in their native tongue. The barber behind my chair was bearded, tall and wide. As he picked up his scissors I noticed slightly tremulous hands that quickly sounded mental alarm bells.

As my scalp became slowly shorn, periodically hairs were frequently and painfully plucked rather than snipped by the unfortunately old and clearly dull scissors. Without the courage to complain under the broad and somewhat unsteady hands of the bearded giant, my reaction became only an occasional involuntary grimace. Mom and dad had walked out to the shop next door so there was no one to call upon for succor. Happily, my shearing was finished first and my parents returned just as Monny had completed his. Deciding that these episodes were probably standard with haircuts out of my own hometown of Cedarhurst, I said nothing. We completed our Sunday beach expedition and returned home, but as we climbed out of the car, mom peered at my scalp and noted scattered red dots in myriad areas. Quickly recognizing the source, she asked me whether I had noticed the plucked scalp and multiple crimson follicles that my cap had covered after the giant barber had completed what was surely his first haircut. Explaining that I had not wanted to annoy the huge man with unsteady hands and had planned to simply stick it out until the plucking was done. Then I told mom that I'd like to continue haircutting, always and forever, only with the nice barber in our hometown. After hearing that explanation, she kissed me and agreed.

The second of only two unpleasant beach experiences occurred three years later when we drove to the beach on a cloudy day in August. We decided not to settle on the sand as the sky continued to cloud. Because it was still warm and we were unsure about possible rain, dad suggested we'd enjoy Nathan's hot dogs until the sky disclosed our immediate future. Wisely, he decided that five frankfurters was insufficient for three boys plus mom and dad, even though each roll was laden with mustard and relish along with our usual sodas of celery tonic, so he doubled the order and added French fries. Of course it was barely enough for three boys but mom suggested we might take a walk along the boardwalk and then if our appetites demanded, the three sons could later enjoy ice cream cones.

As we continued our stroll along the boardwalk, we looked down to the beach and saw two men and two ponies in a fairly large ring of poles planted in the sand. A single rope encircling the ring connected them. At one end the horses were tethered to poles beside the men. Periodically, the boardwalks had a wide staircase down to the beach and the horsemen wisely had set up their ring adjacent to one. Neither of my brothers was at all interested in horseback riding but Tom Mix of movie fame was a special hero of mine. Enthusiastically, I implored dad to let me ride the pony in the ring just like my hero would. Once before, at about age three, a picture had been taken while the pony stood motionless with me on his back, but I had never actually ridden a moving real live horse.

We all went down the stairs to the beach and dad negotiated a ride a few times within the ring for me. The owner, seeing that the smallest of the three boys was to be the horseman, selected the smaller of the two already saddled steeds, then hoisted me onto his back while he was still attached to the post. Then, slipping the bridle and reins from the post, he moved it over the pony's head and handed the reins to me. Ordinarily, the pony would trot around the roped ring a few times, stopping at the attachment poles each time until the owner slapped his rump and started him on another circle. The pony circled again to the far end, but for unknown reason the post there had pulled out of the sand leaving a large gap in the ring. When the pony saw the opening, he suddenly perked up and increasing his stride, dashed out of the ring and broke for the ocean edge where the sand was firm and more readily trod upon than the soft deep sand.

Certain I was going to fall off the galloping pony and die, and forgetting completely about my hero, Tom Mix, I let the reins go and grabbed the pommel, holding on for dear life as the pony found new freedom, clearly planning never to return to an enclosed rope ring again. For me, as a totally new experience, this result caused sheer panic. Suddenly there was a high-pitched somewhat familiar voice sounding much like a panicky eight year old, shouting, "Get me off of this dumb horse!" Of course I was the one repeatedly shouting, "Get me off this dumb horse! Get me off this dumb horse!" What other language could be expected from the unrefined vocabulary of an eight-year old?

Mom's blood pressure must have risen unsparingly – many years later it was part of her ultimate undoing. But all I could do was continue to shout as we splashed along the ocean's edge. One of the two horsemen in the ring mounted the remaining horse and galloped after us as other beach goers, who had chosen to walk along the water's edge, jumped out of our way. As my pony approached the jetty, he saw he was unable to progress further because of the high rocky barrier. He skidded to an abrupt halt, unable to turn seaward or back up onto the deep sand. I was holding so tightly to the pommel that the sudden skid happily failed to unsaddle me. Almost simultaneously, the wrangler pulled up and grasped the bridle and bit, quickly managing to control my unhappy mount and its equally unhappy rider. It took a while before either of the three us became settled. "Calm" was not the current characterization for neither the pony nor me.

Both panicky parents and my two brothers, having seen this mini-stampede from afar, were breathlessly approaching the area where the wrangler, together with the jetty barrier, had saved the day. Both brothers were very close, followed many yards back by dad. Poor mom was a great distance back and breathless.

How did this fiasco end? Well, dad got his money back – I remember that. Mom continued virtually breathless almost all the way home. Both brothers, after realizing that their dumb little brother was OK, thought it had been a great adventure and secretly were a little jealous. No one in my immediate family ever suggested horseback riding again. But – the very next Saturday couldn't come quickly enough. We waited in the movie house for the next cowboy feature to begin because that's when my friends would hear my special version of my story of the exciting adventure. And indeed they were all impressed by the description of the airborne horse's four-legged gallop over and onto the wet sand after bolting through his surrounding rope-and-wooden ring on the beach. Together, the pony and I had splashed all the way to the jetty, the only barrier remaining after his escape. There, as an expert equestrian, I had brought the runaway steed to a sliding halt. Remaining a horse-riding hero for several years through many subsequent "westerns," I explained many times to all my movie-going friends how similar the movie cowboys roped and lassoed their runaway steeds, virtually as I had at my Atlantic beach horseback adventure.

Decades later when my wife, Alice, and I lived in Colorado, we took many adventurous horseback trips along mountain trails and splashing streams – but that's another story.

MUSTARD
MISHAPS
AND MOVIES OF
CHILDHOOD

Mustard, Mishaps and Movies of Childhood

My growth to adulthood was nothing short of miraculous – at least according to my very protective mother. In the first decade of my childhood, threats to my health and survival were everywhere, but the remedies mom imposed for various afflictions were significantly more painful than the diseases. Even now, when someone passes me the Grey Poupon to place sparingly on my hot dog, I shudder a little. It conjures up the mustard plasters splayed upon my innocent and hairless chest of childhood, because to mom, my minimal cough foretold imminent pneumonia. In mitigation of these assaults, I must remind you that this was an era that preceded antibiotics by decades, and pneumonia in a child was serious indeed.

For those of a later generation let me describe this remedy – a mustard poultice that international law might now forbid to use to torture and extract information from the most heinous enemy spy. Perhaps I exaggerate just a bit, but the powdered "Chinese" mustard in large quantity would be mixed with tap water, then slathered onto a tattered, moistened dishtowel – a towel that had been so well used in the kitchen that it became a diaphanous gauze that could no longer serve its original purpose. It was then folded over to cover the noxious slurry and placed upon the victim's chest. (I was going to say 'patient's' chest but victim is probably more accurate). The intention was to stimulate coughing and expectorating – and to "draw" to the surface whatever evil occupied the lungs. What it actually did, however, was turn the skin bright red and caused a hot and fiery sensation. Sufficiently intense burning occurred to nullify mother's promise of the ice cream that she offered if only I would tolerate it for more than two minutes. Unheeded went my suggestion that we use the ice cream on my chest instead of the mustard plaster. In retrospect, perhaps it worked for I did not "come down" with pneumonia, although the redness (that today one might label "first degree burns") persisted for hours.

Alas! The following winter a microscopic organism did indeed choose my chest as a temporary residence. Awakening during the night with a deep and resonant cough, I alarmed a sleeping mother. The rectal thermometer, which in that era had not yet been refined enough for the oral route, found its way first to the Vaseline jar, then immediately into my nether regions, emerging with a Fahrenheit number that prompted mother to make an immediate phone call to our family doctor.

I was grateful that there was sufficient maternal angst to bypass the homeopathic mustard plaster. Dr. Robbins took care of all of us, my mother and dad, my two brothers and me, and I'm sure he'd have prescribed for the family dog if necessary – and he usually made a house call. Indeed, he arrived on this snowy winter day within an hour of the summons and promptly unsheathed his stethoscope. Then to my eternal gratitude, the kindly and considerate medic slid the ice-cold metal and plastic auscultation end under his jacket and against his shirt, to warm it before applying it to my back to hear my crackling lungs.

What he heard evidently called for immediate action for he went to the traditional black bag and extracted a soft leather folder. Happily, nothing with sharp edges or points emerged. Instead, there were a dozen small round bottles about three inches in depth and half that in diameter. He explained to me that there was to be a trial by fire. Then to my great relief he explained that the primary heated object was not to be me but rather to be the small bottles. He placed them in neat rows on my chest, and by heating them ever so slightly, it drove the room air out of them thus creating a vacuum. The suction at the mouth of each bottle then pulled at my skin. The rows of little round red mounds that were produced were visible evidence of the efficacy of the vacuum, and were thought to relieve the congestion in my lungs. The intervention may have had little to do with my recovery but mom immediately felt better. This, combined with a prescribed cherry-flavored elixir, bed rest and ample intake of (what else could it have been) – chicken soup – brought me through.

Mom also explained and cautioned me against many additional threats to children's well-being other than microorganisms that one had to be wary of – especially if no one first warned you about them. The dangers of an open umbrella in the house – even to let it dry out – foretold a future fraught with peril – a peril that was almost as hazardous as tossing your hat carelessly to lie on the bed, rather than hanging it up. Should the misfortune occur of popping a button from my shirt (not an unusual occurrence for a preteen boy) mother was willing to sew it back, but only if I kept the shirt on, and only if I would also chew (on nothing) vigorously, until the repair was completed. This assured her that my immature brain would not suffer the facsimile of the tightly sewn adhesions on whatever garment she was repairing as I wore it.

One of the most hazardous undertakings occurred on the rainy Saturdays when my brother and I each were provided with a nickel for candy and the fifteen-cent movie plus two dimes back and forth for the bus – a grand total of forty cents. Permit me to digress for a moment about these Saturday matinees. Things were different in small towns in the 1930s. Guessing nowadays, a ten and a twelve-year-old boy would not be permitted to take a twenty-five minute ride on a many-stops-local bus to the far off movie theater all by themselves. The bus fare from our corner was indeed ten cents each way. But we had secret plans for our (then genuine) 90% silver dimes treasure plus the extra nickels. If we walked several more blocks to the next bus zone, the fare became only a nickel, providing us with two extra nickels (provided we took the long walk both going and returning). And that meant we could stray from the final destination bus stop near the theater a mere half block to "The Nickel Palace!"

Ah, The Nickel Palace – even in those days the gustatory fare served at this gourmet emporium was priced incredibly low. Five cents purchased a hot dog composed of whatever meat-like ingredients that had been left entirely to the imagination. But to preteens it was the color, texture and spicy flavor in a doughy bun that in turn enclosed green relish and bright yellow mustard. And the condiments were splashed ad lib to a volume that almost exceeded the elongated object it covered, thus challenging our cast iron stomachs.

And what beverage accompanied this dubious sandwich? Why, another Indian-head nickel was all that was needed to acquire the ideal accompaniment – sweet cold nectar of the gods – the creamy textured but cream-devoid chocolatish "milk"shake. How we survived this repast and added the Dots or Milk Duds or Black Crows from the candy and popcorn counter at the theater was only possible because the long return walk left us ready for the more wholesome dinner that our unsuspecting mom prepared.

Innocently, she believed that her visibly well-nourished offspring had had nothing truly wholesome to eat since lunch. Of course she was naively correct, in terms of real food. And lunch had been a long time ago. It had preceded a cartoon, the next chapter of the weekly serial, a crowing rooster heralding the news report, previews of next week's screen offering and finally, a climactic double feature.

But wait! I've digressed from the menace to health that the rainy afternoon at the movies threatened. Of course it was necessary that small boys walking in the rain must step in and splash as many puddles that the fractured sidewalk presented. Mother was aware of that probability and knew that advising against it was hopeless, so she insisted we wear our rubbers over our shoes. A few of the more cautious mothers insisted upon galoshes with careful snaps that closed to a higher level so splashes would not penetrate socks from the bottom of the standard knickers to ankles.

However there were new hazards under these conditions. She and many other mothers in the neighborhood believed with absolute certainty that wearing rubbers while watching the flickering screen in the movie theater caused "weak eyes," and if done repeatedly, blindness was inevitable. So we were admonished and repeatedly reminded once seated to take the rubbers off our shoes.

Preceded by exploits of vocalizing cartoon creatures such as canines (e.g. Goofy), poultry (e.g. Donald Duck) and porcine characters (often up to Three Little Pigs), and following three-plus hours of cowboys and Indians the distracted children were absent minded about ancillary footwear. The theater owner had a windfall each week of many varieties of overshoes from forgetful children. Harried mothers stopping by the theater to distinguish precisely which of the identical black rubbers belonged to whose child followed this. Mattering little that they chose, they knew that the next rainy Saturday would afford a new opportunity for an overshoe and rubber exchange. Mothers could search for an appropriate size for their rapidly growing children among the multi-sized and miscellaneous footwear.

Thus were we prepared for the next rainy expedition, if only we could bear to wait an entire week to learn what happened to the intrepid jungle explorers in the serial or the heroic cowboys of the cactus and lead-filled west where the sheriff always won.

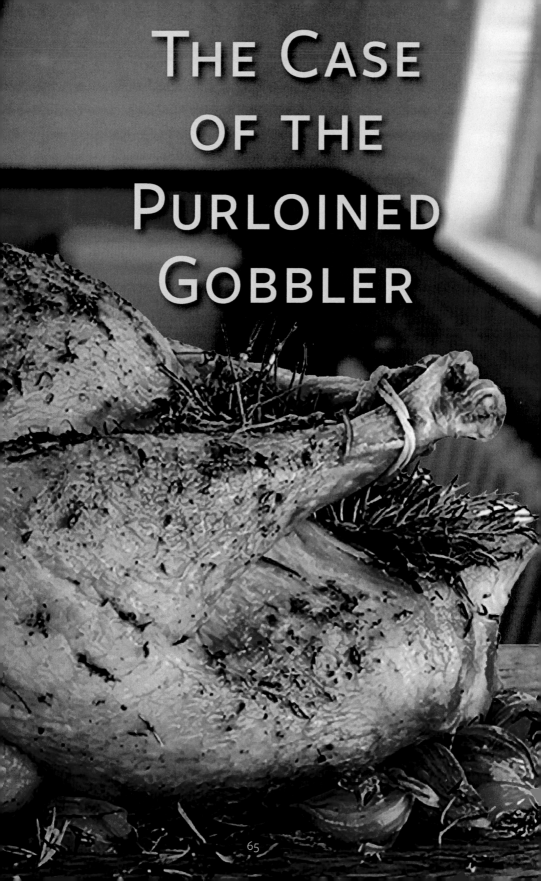

THE CASE OF THE PURLOINED GOBBLER

THE CASE
OF THE PURLOINED GOBBLER

In my preteen years, it was a tradition for our family to welcome many of our close friends and relatives to our house on Long Island for Thanksgiving celebration. The scene could have been adapted from a Woody Allen movie. There was dad's sister, Aunt Minnie, and her husband Uncle Al. Dad tolerated Uncle Al only because he was also the father of Aunt Minnie's children. Uncle Al was a band musician who travelled widely and often, leaving Minnie and my cousins, Bernie and Billie, too frequently with insufficient funds for sustenance. Dad was called upon often for temporary financial help – help that was seldom temporary.

Norman was dad's partner in the dress business. His wife, Betty, was best known as the community gossip. Once unobserved, I heard her report to mom, sotto voce, which of the husbands from their ladies mah-jong group were cheating. Retrospectively, as a preteen child, my naive assumption was that she was referring to slight of hand at the pinochle games the fathers frequently played on Sunday afternoon. Their kids, Milton and Rita, were about the age of my two older brothers. At nineteen jaded years, Rita was much too old and sophisticated to consort with me, an eleven-year old. Milton simply enjoyed punching me in the arm at any opportunity if no adult was looking.

Aunt Clara was the family Cassandra, albeit lacking the mythical beauty. Inevitably, she foresaw doom in all impending events, especially upcoming weddings in the family when she deplored the mate-to-be, either bride or groom – whichever was to join the family. Uncle Max, my father's younger brother and Clara's incredibly tolerant husband, was afflicted with Paget's Disease and was unable to function well, even as an employee of my father at the wholesale dress business. By good fortune, however, there was my Aunt Tillie, a tiny sprightly woman, mom's younger sister, who loved to talk and play with my brother and me. Her husband, Dave, in the fur-coat business, had some of the same lightness of being.

But in my youthful judgment, unabashedly influenced by appetite, there was no significant competition for bachelor Uncle Charlie. Favorite Uncle Charlie was a gentle man, slight of stature and of rotund configuration with wattles surpassed only by the guest of honor, the turkey. His eyesight left much to be desired as witnessed by the saucer-sized lenses he wore with magnification that transfigured his entire physiognomy into that of a benevolent owl. He won a place in our greedy little hearts because he could always be depended upon to escort all the kid cousins to Raeder's drug store cum ice cream shop for a summer afternoon treat.

The adventure I will relate took place on a crisp autumn afternoon as the wind blew crackling leaves about the yard and stacked them against the red bayberry hedge. The pilgrims arrived in fits and starts to join us in what was anticipated to be a convivial soiree featuring Meleagris gallopavo, the non alcoholic version of Wild Turkey, long since domesticated for family feasting.

Because of the large number of celebrants, special arrangements at table were necessary. Adults were to be seated at the dining room table that had been extended by the maximum number of leaves, but even then could not seat us all. Jealously, I noted my big BIG brother and cousin Rita were counted among the adults. To my dismay, a card table was aligned with the main table but it extended through a diminished doorway, well beyond the dining room into the adjacent living room. The card table bridged the doorsill, leaving no doubt that some of us were adjudged beyond the pale, unquestionably isolated. This was the children's table. At the adjoining ends of the dining table and our lesser table, the seats were placed back to back. Could there be any more blatant indication of our exclusion?

But worse news was yet to come. My brother and I had as a table partner, Milton of the flailing knuckles! I did not wish to add additional trauma to my upper arm that already shone with variegated black, blue and red color from prior contact. This was too much to bear. Shunted from the festivities, my brother and I sought redress. Appealing to our parents to squeeze the guests closer to make room for two scrawny, narrow and neglected children bought no sympathy. Their alternative offer was for us to skip the feast altogether – an incredibly heartless gibe. My brother and I turned our hearts and minds inward and found the darkest solution to the dilemma, kidnapping! Or more accurately, turkey-napping.

While the adults socialized in the living room, we reconnoitered the true activity zone, the kitchen. After roasting, the turkey was momentarily abandoned for cooling, in order to render it suitable for dismembering and apportionment. No one was on guard as we crept silently up to the pedestal supporting the sacrificial cutting board upon which the object of our worship lay resplendent. Grasping the handles on each end of the cutting board with which it had been so providentially provided, we snatched the twenty-five pounder away and hastily began the ascent of the staircase.

After only a step or two we came to appreciate the way a newly constructed ship is launched. The oleaginous bird made it unnecessary to grease the skids. Ever present gravity and the inclined plane of staircase and cutting board launched our turkey thumpingly down the few steps to the landing. Happily unwitnessed by any other eyes, we secured the bird by neck and legs and more cautiously carried it to the hideaway we had carefully chosen in advance. We thought we had cleverly considered the vantage point from which we could best bargain for a place at the table. Nothing suited us better than the upstairs bathroom, complete with sink, toilet and a door that locked. With those utilities and a turkey, we avowed we could hold out forever! We dusted the turkey, carefully picking off the larger pieces of carpet lint by hand, but decided against rinsing it in the tub or shower.

It was not long before we heard stirrings below that indicated our desperate action had aroused some attention. "Boys," we heard our mother call. "Freddy and Monroe, where are you?" Wanting to begin negotiations as soon as possible, we opened the door just wide enough to respond before locking down tight again.

"Mom. We're here, upstairs."
"Where is the turkey?"
"Here."

Filtering through her voice I heard a note of despair or possibly anguish but most likely exasperation. Then I heard her call, "Dave."

Knowing we were going to get down to business now that my father had entered the scene, I had momentary qualms as I heard him ascending the steps much more rapidly than usual. It occurred to me that this might not be an easily negotiated peace process. Several hard knocks on the door accompanied by, "Come out of there right now," heralded second thoughts about the entire venture. My big brother was struck dumb by the fiery tone of my father's command, so I answered, "Can we sit at the big table?" I still believed it was a fair exchange, the justice of which I was sure reasonable people anywhere would appreciate. Father, at that moment, apparently could not be included among the cadre of reasonable people. It was in certain terms that he responded, "I'm taking my belt out."

What this meant precisely was obscure because we had never before challenged this threat. It was the ultimate statement signifying that dad had reached the end point of tolerance for our mischief. Yet somehow the revolutionary in me continued the protest. "We don't have to come out," I said. "We have food and water and a toilet."

Beginning to think beyond the next few hours and considering that we might have taken this a step too far, a capitulation now conceivably would be a more prudent resolution – better than spending the next several days in the fortress until dad had to go to work when the holiday was over. After a brief parlay with my brother, who had long since appreciated the folly of this adventure, I stated, "We'll come out if you won't spank us." Dad growled a simple, "OK." I should have recognized his tone as one that did not suggest a generous recognition of justice in our proviso. Generally knowing him to be a man of his word, I trustingly unlocked the door. Oh the perfidy!

First the turkey was rescued as my big BIG brother swooped in, grabbed the bird and scrambled downstairs to mom, waiting to assuage the restive horde below who were unaware of the drama transpiring over their very heads. This delayed only for a moment the wrath of the affronted as my beet-faced father descended upon us. He was not armed with the fearful belt as he had threatened. It was not necessary. Sufficient impression was made by a single spank respectively to the nether regions of my brother and me to convince us of the evil of our ways. He sent us to bed, an even crueler fate at four in the afternoon. We wondered if the guests had noticed our absence or made an inquiry – or if perforce the story had been exposed in elucidating our abstinence from the familial Thanksgiving celebration.

Our appetites had not been abated by the adrenaline-inspiring sequence of events and we also had some concern about further retribution after the guests had left. We considered asking Aunt Tillie for asylum until all wrath was spent or healed by time. By seven O'clock, hunger pangs had increased dramatically. We lay there in bed reflecting upon the error of our ways – not error in stealing the turkey, but rather whether we could have negotiated differently with more favorable results. Just as we were sure we would expire from hunger and malnutrition and certain we would be leaving our parents sobbing with grief about the way we had been abused, mom came up to our room bearing a large tray with two dishes replete with turkey, stuffing, cranberries and wonder of wonders, two full glasses of milk and pumpkin pie covered with whipped cream. We never asked about dad's opinion.

THE
GOOD HUMOR
MAN

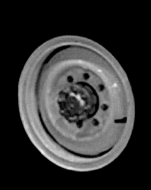

THE GOOD HUMOR MAN

In the 1930s, the south shore of Long Island was not covered with as much concrete and asphalt as may be found there today. There were small forests and open fields with tall grass for a youngest brother like me to explore – as jungle explorer, cowboy or pirate – whatever was the chosen role of the day. But poor Monny! He was the middle of the three brothers and burdened by sensitivity to so many of the varieties of foliage through which we crept together. Brushing across the prevalent poison ivy, oak or sumac (several of whose surfaces wept their oily urushiol) was sufficient to cause his skin to blossom, crimson and crusty.

For him on more than one occasion, the eruption was enough to warrant several days at home, first in bed and then ambulatory before returning to school after the rash had finally subsided. Unlike the previous legacy of measles, which I had inherited from him, this dermatologic rash wasn't contagious for me. We had no knowledge of the chemistry of this itchy, leafy ubiquitous demon. Experience taught us to avoid the triple-leafed shiny ivy. We weren't sure about which of the oak or sumac varieties were noxious and also to be shunned. Many years later I learned that the Japanese had made clever use of their esoteric botanic knowledge by including urushiol, a Japanese defined word for a plant substance that causes a rash, into the lacquer they used when plating gold leaf on the golden Temple in Kyoto. Thieves, who had no knowledge of urushiol, were certain the gods had discouraged them from scraping the gold from the surfaces, knowing they might later be literally caught red-handed, if they too were allergic to urushiol.

This summertime experience occurred when my brother again unhappily suffered sufficient dermatologic affliction to remain in bed. Had it occurred during the school year, skipping classes would have been a consummation devoutly to be wished, but to take to his bed in summer he had to be thoroughly miserable. In those days, the only remedy of which we were aware was a skin application called calamine lotion. To a great degree, it palliated the itching but no curative value was apparent. Time plus the body's intrinsic defenses became the path to normality of uncrusted skin again.

The lotion did provide comic relief, probably not for my brother but certainly for me. After painting onto his reddened face this sometime-white-and- sometime-pink liquid, our joint playtime choices became twofold and afforded my imagination free reign. We could choose to be the bane of the cowboy's existence – the pink war-painted Indian Warrior, or alternatively to convert the bedroom that we shared into a circus tent. It was nolo contendere because the calamine lotion soon turned to a powdered facial mask of which any circus performer would be proud. The task then was to bring frogs, turtle and salamanders up from the basement laboratory to provide a proper sideshow menagerie. We lacked a marching band but a musical miracle suddenly became upon us. The jingling melodies of the itinerant ice cream vendor pervaded the air – the Good Humor man! Even more astonishing: he quickly drove up our driveway and into our very own 40 Maple Avenue backyard double garage!

Only moments later I became aware of the current doings of my oldest BIG brother. Being eight years my senior, he usually disregarded me and my activities. Having been graduated from High School just before the summer began and not unlike several of his classmates, he was currently unemployed and with time on his hands. One of their activities to remedy the ennui that overtakes unoccupied teens, was an occasional poker game, strictly out of the purview of parents. Stakes sometimes rose to enormous sums, sometimes approaching nearly a dollar! Such a degenerate afternoon had been planned for a foursome but initially it had not included Norman. He was the more ambitious graduate who had signed on to the mobile frozen treat company. A persistent rain had discouraged the ice cream-seeking junior populace from the curbs and Norman belatedly responded to the earlier invitation from big BIG brother to attempt a less secure but potentially more remunerative pursuit.

There, literally in my own backyard, stood a prize that had been coveted for many years – a whole ice cream truck! What ten-year old could ever have a lifetime dream fulfilled at such an early stage in his treasure-seeking career? The puzzle now became how best to profit from this windfall. How to get past the gamblers (now including the truck-driving huckster) all of whom sat between me and the back door to the driveway and the garage? There was no choice but to use a route I had previously employed only when truly necessary to exit my home unnoticed; the bedroom window allowed an easy descent onto the kitchen roof, then to the nearby rain pipe and its spout that was alongside the trellis, attached in turn to the brick wall that led all the way to the ground.

The rain had continued lightly but it was summer and warm. With such incentive ahead mere rainwater was readily shrugged away. Pulling the hinged garage door open – there was no motorized overhead sliding door in those days – and there, gleaming white, was the object of my foray complete with the image of a chocolate ice cream pop, emblazoned in full color on the truck's side door that led to the booty within.

Alas, it was not to be! So close to fulfillment of my dreams only to have them dashed by a padlock on the door! Oh how I bemoaned the untrusting world that was of such a nature to believe an ice cream truck needed to be guarded from thieves! It was much later that the realization came upon me that they had every right to foresee potential incursions upon their priceless property from a younger- than-teen-age malefactor!

But wait! There was a rear door as well! Again, this too was padlocked. To see if somehow the door could be lifted from the hinge side, I climbed on the rear bumper and clung to the roof. Never before had I encountered an aerial view of the Good Humor truck. Lo and behold, the secret was the roof! There was a hatch! Swiftly it became apparent that, although the treats were dispensed by the vendor from side and rear doors, the treasure was loaded through this roof hatch – an aperture that required an effort that taxed a 10 year old almost to the limit, but once penetrated, revealed the glorious bounty below.

Quickly perusing the visible contents from above, a carton was selected that appeared to hold the two dozen favorites that brother and I most enjoyed, the butter-scotch sundae composed of coffee ice cream slathered in viscous sugary butter-scotch topping. Sad though it was to leave behind so many other delicacies, yet knowing I could never hope to explain to mom large boxes of Good Humors should I dare to deposit them in the freezing compartment of the refrigerator, I relinquished the idea of further plunder. Calculating that the mere two-dozen could readily be consumed by my poor sick brother and me, we reckoned that it was barely past midday – and supper was at least five hours away.

Now remained a logistical problem – how to transport the loot, unobserved, past the unsuspecting custodian whose carefully secured and double-locked merchandise had been pilfered. Closing the garage door and speeding through the rain to the cellar door (never locked in those halcyon days of trust) there I descended to my laboratory/workshop. Recovered there was a bushel basket that had been salvaged on my last visit to the grocery store when I accompanied my mother. Hastily placing the carton within (whose contents I feared were slowly melting into a café au lait puddle of cream and sugar) I covered it with a rather disreputable torn towel from the rag bin basket, then placed on top of it the glass tank within which my turtle dwelled when he was not exercising with me.

Mounting the cellar stairs I strode blithely past the den of poker iniquity mounting from street level to the one story above. They paid no attention to me at all, even when I pointedly discontinued my pseudo casual off-key whistling to announce to all that I was carrying my turtle up to visit my poor sick brother in our bedroom. Somewhat disappointed, I became aware that my elaborate subterfuge was totally unnecessary for the quintet was thoroughly preoccupied with slips of numbered and illustrated cardboard.

With great panache I revealed my feat to my bedridden brother as I stripped away the ragged towel, much as a sorcerer might have whisked away his cape. Quickly dispelling all doubt I unveiled my prize to the harlequin-faced invalid who had skeptically awaited the conclusion of my venture. Concluding my heroic descent and triumphant return upstairs, we set ourselves the task of making the ill-gotten gains in the four and twenty still chilled vessels totally disappear.

Mother couldn't understand, when 6 O'clock rolled around, why neither of us had our usual appetite for one of our supremely cherished dishes – split pea soup with savory disks of frankfurters floating therein. Nor did we have any reasonable explanation for two kitchen teaspoons upstairs.

MR. GUTTMAN'S
CANDY STORE

MR. GUTTMAN'S CANDY STORE

Central Avenue was the main street that ran through the Five Towns on southern Long Island. Our local shops were all within an easy walk, about a block and a half from our home on Maple Avenue. The Rensey Drug and Ice Cream Store (owned by Mr. Yesner - which was Rensey spelled backwards) plus Mr. DeGillio's barbershop, and Mr. Dinces' Children's Clothing shop (whose son, Eugene was my classmate at P.S.# 3) but most important to me, was Mr. Guttmann's candy store. Our families utilized all four establishments, but the candy store was the one we kids most frequently visited. It had opened in 1938 when I was ten years old, and it was the shop where a penny could always buy something. Most of my friends and I usually had up to a nickel and rarely a dime. It could take each of us as much as fifteen minutes to decide whether we would use our pennies one-by-one or splurge on the many more costly objects to savor, for as much as two to five cents each. Fortunately, Mr. Guttmann was endowed with infinite patience when he had opened his candy store, having happily emigrated from Germany to the US several years before World War II began. There were also many more complex sweets than those we enjoyed as children, but only adults could afford to buy the large boxes of Whitman's and See's candy for Anniversaries, Birthdays and other special occasions.

The War was not even a year underway following the Pearl Harbor bombing by Japan in 1941 and Germany's declaration of war on us. But seventy-six years ago, teenagers were significantly much less informed than they are now from newspapers, TV, and hand held iPad or iPhone. In those days, we were pleased that war had not cut off our candy supply, although prices had increased by several pennies over the intervening years. When we had completed the schoolday classes and as usual were en route to Mr. Guttmann's store, we were quite surprised to see two police cars parked at the curb out in front – and even more taken aback to see the shop's door sign said, "closed."

Of course we walked up to the open window of the one black and white car that still had a policeman inside, where he was sitting in the passenger seat. Our questions flew, asking if Mr. Guttmann was OK and what about his wife? We had been aware for a long time that she had been sickly, and both Mr. and Mrs. had always lived in the back rooms behind the store itself. The policeman gave us a pleasant smile and told us he couldn't answer any questions yet, but both Mr. and (the unwell) Mrs. Guttmann had been taken to the police station. His fellow officers were currently carrying out searches and other important police activities in the store. When one of us explained that we had come for our usual afternoon candy and then asked how soon might we go in and select it, he replied that the store was now closed and he had no idea when – or if – it would ever be opened again. "Remember," he reminded us, "We're at war with Germany." We weren't sure exactly what he meant by that or how it was related to candy. Soon it was clear that we were going to learn nothing more from him, so we said goodbye and walked away down the block. After a discussion among us we decided to head home and explain to our mothers, brothers and sisters about the exciting police adventure in which we had participated. Later towards evening, when most fathers had come home from work, we repeated the unusual happenings again. My parents listened closely but chose not to offer any explanations. I heard them speaking together about it afterwards, but much too softly to overhear.

My brothers and I had become too busy with school preparing for finals and various other essential teen activities, when four days after the candy store incident, our teacher brought the New York Daily News to class to show us a two column story a few pages inside the paper. It was lengthy and amusingly critical of the Nassau County and local police. Large print led the two-column episode with:

German Refugees Arrested
Crippled Wife Hospitalized

Just four days ago, without warning, two police squads burst into the candy store on Central Avenue in Cedarhurst, arrested the elderly owner and his bedridden wife and brought them handcuffed to the local Police Station into holding-cells.

Within a very short time, three volunteer Lawyers arrived, each sharing the burden of bail after the local judge determined that the Guttmanns were no threat to the citizens of Cedarhurst, Nassau County, New York State or the United States of America.

This is how it all began.

The Guttmanns had escaped from Germany as Jewish refugees in the late 1930s. Not long after their arrival in the US, poor Mrs. Guttmann becme increasingly afflicted with severe rheumatoid arthritis – so crippling that she could barely walk. Mr. Guttmann, her husband of many years, continued to care for her as he always had, as a childless but a long and happily married couple. With the aid of other immigrants, many of who had already been in the US long enough to become citizens, he had borrowed sufficiently to set up his candy store. Behind, but directly attached to the candy store, was their small home, complete with bed room, living room, small dining room, bathroom with tub and shower and amply equipped kitchen. As with all the other shops, the back doors led to an alley wide enough for autos and trashcans. As a few years went by, Mrs. Guttmann's rheumatism became worse and she became increasingly unable to ambulate, limited almost always to their small house when she completely stopped helping in the candy store. Because of the distance from shop-front to home-bedroom, Mr. Guttmann invested in an intercom so the two could communicate; either for help when necessary or just to speak with each other when the shop became less busy. It was the intercom plus simple stupidity that led to the police raid.

Remember, when this unfortunate episode occurred, the US had been at war with Germany for less than a year, following Pearl Harbor's successful and catastrophic bombing by Japan. There continued to be concern among adults (and less knowledge among kids) that the US mainland might soon be attacked or even invaded. What was the information that had been passed on to the local police that had stimulated an armed raid on the little shop? The newspaper story continued with the information that had led to the raid.

It explained the source of the false description given to the local police by a misin-
formed citizen of Cedarhurst who had sought a box of candy from Mr. Guttmann's
shop for his wife's birthday. As he was purchasing the candy from the owner, he
heard a heavily German accented voice coming from an intercom behind the counter. The customer thought he heard the foreigner commenting words to the effect,
"We Germans are ready to launch as soon as we can, before it gets too cold." Leaving the candy box un-purchased on the counter and almost running down the street
to the Police Station he told the desk officer what he had heard. He then had to
repeat it several times until he reached the Lieutenant in charge. The Lieutenant,
who had been fairly recently promoted from a different precinct many miles away,
thought this was a great opportunity for him to progress even faster to Captain.
From the local citizen's information he decided that he should rapidly raid and arrest these local German spies and confiscate their secret radio before whatever was
going to be "launched" would cause citizen's deaths or at least serious damage from
whatever the weaponry was that was about to be launched.

The article continued until its embarrassing conclusion.

As the Lieutenant initiated
the raid it became clear to the
regular local officers (most of
whom were thoroughly familiar with the store and its local
owners) that their new Chief
from far away had made an
error by assuming that the
rapid and incorrect conclusion by the suspicious citizen
had been completely misun-
derstood.

The intercom (*not* long distance *international radio* as
police assumed) was simply
the best way a partially crip-
pled women and her loving
husband could communicate
when separated. The over

heard phrase, "We Germans are ready to launch as soon as we can, before it gets too cold," was actually a message from Mrs. Guttmann to her husband letting him know she had prepared their lunch soup and it was best to come back and eat it before it became cold.

Of course, before the news had become public, the Guttmanns had long since been released and all charges had been dropped – perhaps they had never even been made once the DA heard of the premature actions by the overanxious new police Lieutenant. (He never did make it to Captain). Their business improved after the publicity about how their immigration had occurred only a short time ago, not very long before Hitler began steadily increasing persecution of Jews from Germany (and later, from many other non-German ethnic groups in Europe). After the news of their arrest (and release) became public, a local citizen's committee took up a collection and more than five hundred dollars were presented to the Guttmanns. All this information was virtually incomprehensible for us kids. What was clear to us was that soon after their store reopened, Mr. Guttmann had a special for children – five Hershey's Kisses for a penny.

A Kiss for You